Animators

ABSTRACT

Childhood has changed rapidly over the past few years and the methods that we use as teachers and educators of children and young people should reflect these changes. Children learn best and most when they enjoy what they are doing. Using animation as a tool to encourage and develop children's learning is not only fun but effective! This thesis presents the Animation as an effective learning tool. The very common definition of Animation is representation of images to create an illusion of movement. If I draw a series of images, showing a man walking with each picture having one specific position of his leg movement. If we show these entire set of images one after other real quick, the man magically seems to move! This is the basic ideology behind animation. The project start with research work dealing with the understanding of animation, colours used in a particular scenes where one is trying to focus, psychological behaviour of colours and its impact on viewer. In movie's colour graphics use of colours is very clear, intensity of colours are used in such a way that it doesn't distract the person watching it or disturb the person in some mean and which looks amusing to the viewer. Colour graphics in any movie, whether with living character or animated describe the scenes with talk between the character, their motion and the scenery means background. Many times it's the scenery which attract the people and also character looks beautiful in that scenery. But it's very important to their intensity of which is used as a more informal knowledge source and understanding the problem of students awareness and their attitude towards the computer graphics and how they use it to increase their knowledge about the animation, graphics and specially colour graphics and it challenges the psychology behind understanding the things if taught with help of graphics or motion of pictures. The research trying to state that basic things and general information can be shown or told directly but through animation or graphics specially colour graphics it leaves a mark on people's mind and it is interesting and it's easy to understand if taught with a better understanding of colours and way animation should be represented, so nobody gets bored and student enjoy watching it.

CONTENTS

List of Figures -- i
1. Introduction --- 1
1.1 Problem statement --- 1
1.2 Objective of work --- 1
2. Review Literature --- 2
3. Methodology -- 3
3.1 Does animation an effective learning tool? --- 3
3.2 Animation in making --- 3
    3.2.1 The 2D production pipeline --- 4
        3.2.1.1 script --- 4
        3.2.1.2 Storyboard --- 4
        3.2.1.3 Designs --- 4
        3.2.1.4 Leica Reel (Animatic) -- 4
        3.2.1.5 Pencil Tests (Animation) -- 4
        3.2.1.6 Clean-up -- 5
        3.2.1.7 Inking --- 5
        3.2.1.8 Checking --- 5
        3.2.1.9 Compositing -- 5
        3.2.1.10 Final Edit --- 5
    3.2.2 The Principles of Animation --- 5
        3.2.2.1 Squash and Stretch --- 5
        3.2.2.2 Anticipation -- 6
        3.2.2.3 Staging --- 6
        3.2.2.4 Straight Ahead and Pose to Pose ----------------------------------- 7
        3.2.2.5 Follow through and overlapping action -------------------------- 8
        3.2.2.6 Slow in and slow out --- 8
        3.2.2.7 Arcs -- 9
        3.2.2.8 Secondary activity -- 9
        3.2.2.9 Timing -- 9
        3.2.2.10 Exaggeration --- 10
        3.2.2.11 Solid Drawing --- 10
        3.2.2.12 Appeal --- 11
    3.2.3 Story for the animation movie --- 11
    3.2.4 Character designing and their value in animation -------------------------- 11
3.3 Cognitive behaviour of students using animation as a learning tool ----------- 13
3.4 colours significance in illustrations planning -- 13
3.5 Psychological properties of colours -- 20
3.6 Perceptual salience vs Thematic Relevance -- 24
3.7 Composition of images in animation --- 25
3.8 Detail procedure for animating the story -- 30
                                                                   3.8.1 Story   30
    3.8.2 Adobe flash: Animation software --- 31
3.9 Result --- 34
5. Conclusion --- 35
References --- 36

LIST OF FIGURES

3.2.2.1 Examples of extreme use of squash and stretch ---6
3.2.2.3 Difference between Poor staging and Good staging --- 7
3.2.2.4 Men walking and his feet when he is up, down and contact edge--- 7
3.2.2.6 Overlapping action of men when speed up and lower the speed 3.2.2.9 --- 9
3.2.2.10 timing is maintained according to the sequence of scene and motion--- 10
3.2.5.1 Extracting of an action to enhance and make it more convincing 3.2.5.2 --- 10
3.2.5.2 Change in character value when beard is added, which gives it the value of a grown person---11
3.2.5.3 Front view and side view of character--- 11
3.2.5.4 Blind person with dark specs showing the loss of vision with no expression--- 12
3.2.5.5 Square mentioned in the story and traffic signal--- 12
3.4.1 Warm colours--- 13
3.3.2 Red (primary colour) --- 14
3.3.3. Orange (secondary colour) --- 14
3.3.4 Dark orange picture in lime green background--- 15
3.3.5 Dark orange picture in pink background--- 15
3.3.6 Dark orange picture in dark red background--- 16
3.3.7 Cool colours--- 16
3.3.8 Yellow (primary colour) --- 17
3.3.9 Green (secondary colour)--- 17
3.3.10 Blue (primary colour)--- 17
3.3.11 Purple (secondary colour) --- 18
3.183.12 Neutral colours--- 18
3.3.13 Black: Strongest neutral colour --- 19
3.5.1 RED, Physical --- 19
3.5.2 BLUE. Intellectual --- 20
3.5.3 YELLOW. Emotional --- 20
3.5.4 Green. Balance --- 21
3.5.5 VIOLET. Spiritual --- 21
3.5.6 Orange --- 21
3.5.7 Pink --- 22
3.5.8 Grey--- 22
3.5.9 Black--- 23
3.5.10 White--- 23
3.5.11 Brown--- 23
3.7.1 Intersecting lines --- 24
3.7.2 Element along the lines --- 25
3.7.3 Natural lines--- 26
3.7.4 Diagonal lines --- 26
3.7.5 Natural frames --- 27
3.7.6 Contrast between subject and background --- 27
3.7.7 Closer look at frame --- 28
3.7.8 Patterns and repetition --- 28
3.7.9 Interrupted pattern --- 29
3.7.10 symmetry --- 29
3.8.2.1 Adobe flash layout --- 32

3.8.2.2 Adobe flash Action Script 3.0 screen ---- 33
3.8.2.3: adobe tools ---- 34
3.8.2.4: Adobe flash timeline ---- 35
3.9: final figure ---- 36

1. INTRODUCTION

In gift world of animation we've all quite technology we'd like to provide animation movies with higher graphics. Animated demonstrations square measure progressively used for presenting the practicality of assorted pc applications, in flick creating for camera work Associate in nursing additional or less additionally in education business as an education tool. Withal, our understanding of whether or not and the way students integrate this technology into their learning methods remains restricted. Although, many studies have examined animated demonstrations' learning potency, this study aims at investigation users initial attitudes towards animated demonstrations. Animation isn't simply the motion of few characters on screen however it's additionally a good medium to form folks perceive the message, particularly young children.

Attitudes concerning data sources play a determinative role for his or her acceptance as a result of Quantitative and qualitative data each will be shown in animation. The recognition of mistreatment animations to assist learners perceive and bear in mind data has greatly inflated since the appearance of powerful graphics-oriented computers and animation creating code. This code permits animations to be made rather more simply and cheaply than hand drawn animation. Previously, ancient animation needed specialised labour-intensive techniques that were each long and big-ticket. In distinction, code is currently offered that creates it doable for individual educators to author their own animations while not the requirement for specialist experience. Lecturers are not any longer restricted to counting on static graphics however will pronto convert them into instructional animations.

During learning of animation and their use as a pc and graphics learning tool that square measure made by mistreatment animation code. the main target is on making a brief animation graphics and a flick and on making the character animation mistreatment animation code and different Softwares to make graphics and character and our main saying is to propose a theory that deals with understanding of things instructed in categories if instructed with facilitate of some quite illustration or through motion of objects or straightforward words through animation. However, primarily the project is additionally involved with researching the core principles and ideas of animation towards showing it's an honest learning tool and understanding a way to apply them to a drawn character so as to make the illusion of life.

1.1 Problem Statement

Proposing a theory which explains that animation can be a great learning tool if it is designed considering cognitive behaviour of human mind so that it can enhance the learning efficiency of children's especially in schools.

1.2 objective of the work

This venture was imaginative to me as I had at no other time endeavoured to make any sort of activity clasps either customary or entire liveliness with portrayals or by utilizing movement programming. Additionally the way that in the wake of examining 3 years in mechanical outline I know less about design and I saw no all the more about liveliness as an approach to present the things. I had the capacity recognize great and terrible activity however I was not ready to clarify why one worked and the other didn't and how it provoke me when a scene doesn't act as I composed. As of not long ago my way to deal with liveliness included just taking a seat at a PC and making development through experimentation, trusting that by consistent tweaking, it would look right inevitably. This is conceivable with PC liveliness as all the artist needs to do is make two postures at specific focuses in time and with activity programming we can do the rest. Making changes in accordance with the timing of individual parts of a character is not simple yet with a measure of practice it is conceivably can be accomplished. An enormous measure of forward arranging is essential. To finish a liveliness, the whole grouping needs to be arranged out and to help manage this methodology artists are required to have a firm handle of the centre standards of activity. This task will help me increase important experience and a much more noteworthy comprehension of movement and how we can utilize activity as a more basic device to use in field of instruction as a learning apparatus. I can then utilize this learning to add to a more organized way to deal with make movement a decent learning apparatus.

2. REVIEW LITERATURE

Kids learn best and most when they appreciate what they are doing. Utilizing movement as a device to empower and add to kids' learning is fun as well as successful! By utilizing movement youngsters create aptitudes capabilities in:

- Story telling

- Visual correspondence

- Cognition, passionate, ethic and stylish angles

- Observation and tactile perspectives

- Concentration

- Problem-comprehending and inventive angles

Research done here propose that when kids are having a ton of fun, they have a tendency to learn better. It's even deductively demonstrated that maintenance of data is higher when it is imparted utilizing both visual and verbal correspondence. I have a solid vibe that movement offers energizing potential outcomes for addressing the needs of 21st century learners. The utilization of movement guideline can altogether upgrade understudies learning if appropriately outlined and actualized.

Current instructive utilization of liveliness propose two fundamental parts in learning. To start with reason for liveliness in scholastics is to satisfy a cognitive capacity. In this part, liveliness are planned to backing understudy's cognitive procedure that at last result in them understanding the topic. Movement can be utilized to make exceptionally energizing and fun livelinesss into which training and preparing can without much of a stretch be consolidated. Educators can likewise utilize activity to show things and ideas outwardly precisely how they need to since they have control of each part of the liveliness. It can be utilized to show how things meet up and cooperate. In science for instance the PC activity can be utilized to show how our nearby planetary group functions, and in math, a PC movement may demonstrate an understudy in what manner can logarithmically control particular mathematical statement. Different subjects, for example, English, outside dialect, music and workmanship can likewise be thought by utilizing movement.

Besides, as a full of feeling learning instrument that pulls in consideration, connect with the learner, and manages inspiration. Such emotional movement preparing is not centred around encouraging perception of any scholarly topic itself and regularly depicts exercises that are intuitive, imaginative, fun and motivational.

Youngsters are entranced by activity and quickens stories and they appreciate the chance to make their own. The innovative capability of activity is huge, and coordinating liveliness exercises into the school educational module offers the likelihood of tapping this possibility to meet a scope of instructive targets.

Instructors are excitedly taking up the opportunities that PC activity offers for delineating element content. Case in point, PowerPoint now has a simple to-utilize activity office that, in the right hands, can create extremely compelling instructive activitys. Since movements can expressly delineate changes after some time (transient changes), they appear to be preferably suited to the instructing of techniques and methodology. At the point when used to present element content, activitys can reflect both the progressions in position (interpretation), and the progressions in structure (change) that are crucial to realizing this sort of topic.

Conversely with static pictures, activitys can demonstrate fleeting change specifically (instead of needing to show it in a roundabout way utilizing assistant markings, for example, bolts and movement lines). Utilizing activitys

rather than static illustrations evacuates the requirement for these included markings so that shows can be easier and less jumbled, as well as more distinctive, connecting with, and all the more naturally fathomed. Furthermore, the learner does not need to decipher the helper markings and attempt to gather the progressions that they compress. Such elucidation and induction may request a level of realistic aptitudes that the learner does not have. With energized delineations, data about the progressions included is accessible to be perused straight from the showcase without the learner expecting to perform mental activity. It's a touch of an embellishment, however it's more like being kissed as opposed to perusing about a kiss.

Exploration prove about the instructive adequacy of movements is blended. Different examinations have looked at the instructive adequacy of static and vivified shows over various substance spaces. While there have been a few discoveries that show beneficial outcomes of activitys on realizing, a few livelinesss challenge the learner's transforming limits different studies have discovered no impacts or even negative impacts. As a rule, it can be inferred that liveliness are not inherently more viable than static illustrations. Maybe, the specific qualities of individual activitys and how they are utilized have key part as an impact of the impacts that they have.

3. METHODOLOGY

3.1 Does animation an effective learning tool?

Decently planned livelinesss can help understudies learn speedier and less demanding. They are likewise brilliant help to educators regarding the matter of clarifying troublesome subjects. The trouble of subjects may emerge because of the association of science or creative energy. For example, the electric current is imperceptible. The operation of electric circuits is troublesome for understudies to comprehend toward the starting. With the help of PC activitys, learning and showing may get to be less demanding, speedier and interesting. In the event that in a class instructor attempt to show something which can be clarified just by a discussion between them. It gets to be extremely troublesome for understudies to think for quite a while and since they are not ready to be on the way fixation breaks and they doesn't appears to be taking after things. So they don't get the things yet in the event that same thing is taught with the assistance of illustrations, hued design or with the assistance of movement of articles on screen either by physically or with the assistance of outline Softwares accessible in business sector. It gets to be straightforward the things when we see things happening before us and it gets to be clear when things with graphical representation are clarified by a voice.

3.2 Animation in making

Energizing a 3D character is a testing undertaking that has been drawn nearer from three fundamental headings. In imaginative 3D liveliness, the illustrator utilizes an assortment of systems, for example, keyframe activity, parameter bend altering, opposite and forward kinematics (IK/FK), and numerous targets transforming to specialty the character stances and movements. In information driven activity (e.g., movement catch), live movement is recorded specifically from a performing artist, digitized, and afterward mapped onto a 3D character. In procedural activity, a computational model is utilized to make and control the movement, e.g., the artist sets conditions for some sort of physical or behavioural re-enactment.

3.2.1 The 2D Production Pipeline

It is critical to see how conventional 2D liveliness is produced from beginning idea to last movie or film. I will then actualize these ideas in the advancement of a strategy and way to deal with making my own particular 2D energized work. Any movies, whether real to life or vivified, oblige a tremendous measure of forward arranging keeping in mind the end goal to be finished. Strategies for delivering energized movies are consistently changing and adjusting, joining more advanced and computerized systems. Then again, the fundamental hidden stages behind the generation pipeline continue as before.

3.2.1.1 Script

The principal and most essential phase of any film creation is the creating of a story. In any case, with energized movies, accentuation is set on the visual scripting of the activity and execution while in a real life film there would be more sympathy toward the dialog.

3.2.1.2 Storyboard

This is the phase where the activities and occasions in the script are envisioned graphically as a consecutive arrangement of pictures. The making of a storyboard permits the executive to identify any issues with the script and to roll out important improvements to improve the story. A great deal of changes are made at this stage as once generation begins, it is much harder and unreasonable to revise botches.

3.2.1.3 Designs

A style and a search must be concurred for all characters, props, foundations and whatever other visual components at this stage. The point is to deliver 'model sheets' for every component. The model sheet for a character would comprise of the last outlines and extents alongside a progression of drawn activity postures which the character is prone to accept amid the movement. The model sheets are then utilized as a source of perspective by the group of artists to help keep the look of the character steady all through.

3.2.1.4 Leica Reel (Animatic)

A Leica Reel, or animatic, is just a taped adaptation of the storyboard altered together to test how the last altered film would play out. This stage takes into consideration the chief to change the timing of every shot, arrangement out activity successions and the soundtrack before the genuine creation starts. It is likewise at this stage that liveliness Layouts are created. This stage can be best clarified by 'This step is utilized as a part of setting up extremes for character to be utilized by the key illustrator. It passes on diverse data to the storyboard as it issues you a thought of the activity needed in the grouping of movement and demonstrates the most amazing character stances in the succession.

3.2.1.5 Pencil Tests (Animation)

Once the animatic and all the liveliness formats are endorsed by the chief, the movement can at last initiate. Utilizing the designs, the artists finish every shot utilizing one of a few accessible movement strategies. They are posture to stance or straight ahead. When an arrangement of liveliness is finished, then it can be checked by either flipping through the pictures or sent off to be printed and transformed into film. This film of the generally drawn liveliness is known as a pencil test.

3.2.1.6 Clean-up

As every artist has their own individual way to deal with drawing, it is the occupation of the clean-up craftsman to verify the illustrators work is predictable as to plan and viewpoint. Artists are urged to attract generally a scrappy style as it results in drawings that catch the "vibe" of movement and additionally the stance. The clean-up craftsman should then take these unpleasant drawings and supplant the scrappy lines with precise ones considering all the unobtrusive points of interest forgot by the illustrator.

3.2.1.7 Inking

When all the "clean" casings of activity have been affirmed by the executive they are hued. Customarily the drawings would be exchanged to thin sheets of acetic acid derivation known as cells. Shading would then be painted onto the back of the cells. Notwithstanding, this methodology we now do digitally.

3.2.1.8 Checking

The checker has the dull employment of verifying each casing of a film is amend before it is gone to the last phases of creation. This includes, amongst different things, checking for broken lines, soil on the acetic acid derivation, painting missteps and spotting mix-ups and imperfections in the character that don't coordinate the plans.

3.2.1.9 Compositing

When checking is finished and the cell affirmed, all the components including movement, foundations and enhancements must be united. Generally, this was done through a cam man, yet can now be done digitally by a printer.

3.2.1.10 Final Edit

This is basically the arrangement of all the completed edges into one long grouping prepared for survey on the silver screen.

3.2.2 The Principles of Animation

One of the points of this undertaking was to pick up a much more prominent information and comprehension of how great character liveliness functions. I needed to approach the movement for this venture in an organized and orderly route with the plan of having the capacity to create solid identity, feeling and activity with no dialogs can be indicated in motion picture and entire portrayal of story with music in foundation. For this I required a considerably more intensive establishing in the standards of movement. Numerous strategies and thoughts were consummated over numerous years in making movement and known as the 12 standards of liveliness.
The 12 standards of activity comprise of:

3.2.2.1 Squash and Stretch

This component makes the deception of weight and volume in a character or article. The sum utilized relies on upon what the specific activity requires. Over the top kid's shows will emphasizes amazing measures of squash and stretch, however a full length film will utilize it all the more unobtrusively and reasonably. This guideline is taking into account the way that even in actuality, unless an item is totally unbending and mechanical, it will distort and change shape when moved. This is flawlessly delineated by the flexing and straightening of an arm where muscles under the skin contract and unwind. This system is utilized as a part of a wide range of character activity from a skipping ball to a basic character running. It is the most imperative component of liveliness that needs to be aced and will be utilized frequently.

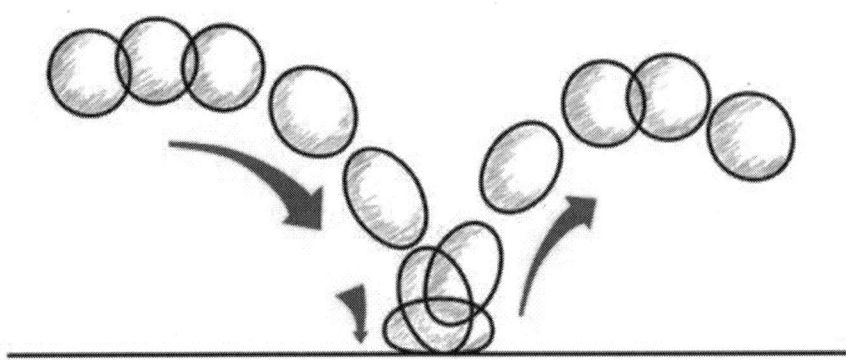

Fig 3.2.2.1: Examples of extreme use of squash and stretch.

3.2.2.2 Anticipation

This is the development that goes before a principle activity, in the same way as key movement. To comprehend what is going on onscreen, there must be an obviously arranged arrangement of activities. Reckoning permits the gathering of people to get ready for what the character is going to do next or with the character conduct on screen there can be forecast of what may be the following scene. It makes tension and uplifts the dramatization or effect of specific activities.

3.2.2.3 Staging

It is the presentation of any thought so it is totally and unmistakably clear. Arranging includes imparting an activity, identity, interpretation or inclination to the gathering of people in the best and direct way conceivable. The fundamental point of an energized film short or long is to recount a story. There is just a constrained measure of time in a film thus it is imperative that every edge help to make the purpose of the story. The activities of the character ought to be clear as can be for the group of onlookers to get it. This is attained to through the situating of the character on screen and how they identify with all other visual components including the foundation, sound and other character and intuitive articles. The activity ought to bode well actually when just viewing the character's profile on screen. Additionally, there ought to be one unmistakable activity at once or else the gathering of people will get befuddled.

Fig 3.2.2.3: difference between Poor staging and Good staging.

3.2.2.4 Straight Ahead and Pose to Pose

There are two primary systems for invigorating known as Straight ahead and Pose to stance. The primary just includes the artist beginning with the first drawing of a succession and energizing it outline by casing until the grouping is finished. There is no genuine learning of how the activity will play out and makes some extremely unique and astonishing results.

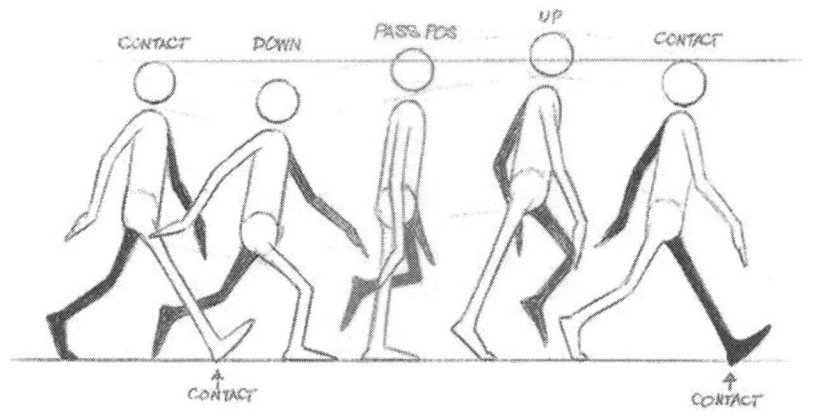

Fig 3.2.2.4: Men walking and his feet when he is up, down and contact edges.

This strategy is utilized just when the illustrator doesn't generally know how to plan an arrangement out. The stance to posture methodology is to plan out key stances in an activity, draw them as best as could be expected under the circumstances and after that do a reversal and attract the great positions. It is then just an issue of making all the edges in the middle of these key postures to make a smooth movement. These in the middle of casings can be passed on to the colleague artist to finish utilizing unmistakably laid out timing directions from the lead illustrator.

Points of interest and burdens of this methodology:

Points of interest:
• Clarity
• The purpose of the scene is clear
• Its well structure technique for working
• Produces great drawings with clear, decipherable positions

- It is in place – the right things happen at the correct time and in the opportune spot
- The executive preferences it
- It is anything but difficult to aid
- It is a faster method for working and authorizes the lead artist to accomplish more scenes

Weaknesses:
- Misses the "stream"
- The activity can get wild and unnatural
- Can be excessively strict
- Misses the "enchantment"

Best way to deal with quickening a scene is through a mix of both strategies. This includes arranging out the activity utilizing little thumbnail portrays. When an arrangement has been thoroughly considered, huge drawings are made of the key activities and after that of whatever other compelling represents that may be helpful. These pictures then go about as aides which the illustrator can go for when really vivifying the grouping. By beginning with the principle assortment of activity the illustrators finishes the shot and afterward retreats over it again including arms and after that again for the head thus on until the whole character is drawn.

Favorable circumstances and inconveniences of this consolidate approach:
Favorable circumstances:
- Combines the organized arranging of the 'stance to-posture' system with the characteristic flexibility of the 'straight ahead' strategy.
- Creates a harmony in the middle of arranging and suddenness
- Creates an essential harmony between inhumanity and energy

Burdens:
- None

3.2.2.5 Follow through and overlapping action

At the point when an individual reaches a stop in the wake of running, they don't just stop. The laws of material science manage that all whatever is left of the body will in any case have force and accordingly will at present be moving. Fusing this thought into liveliness is known as complete. Covering activity happens when a character alters course, however the garments or whatever other limp parts of the body continue taking after the first way of activity. Fundamentally it implies when individual parts of the body need to make up for.

3.2.2.6 Slow in and slow out

This is the ticket of differing the timing and separating between progressive drawings to make activities accelerate and back off. Less drawings between two postures make the activity speedier and more drawings make it slower. Moderate in and moderate out makes a more characteristic and sensible movement when executed effectively. Moderate in can likewise be considered as deceleration, moderate out as increasing speed.

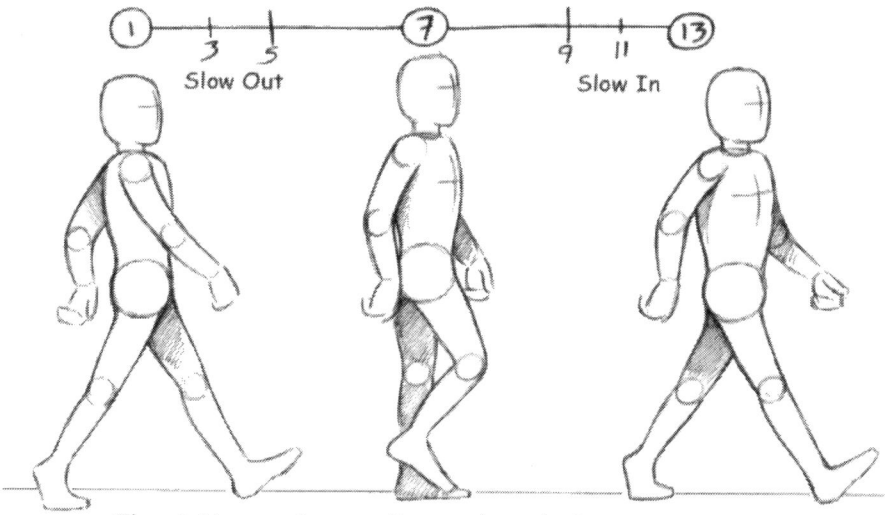

The stride speeds up as it goes through the passing position
Fig 3.2.2.6: overlapping action of men when speed up and lower the speed.

3.2.2.7 Arcs

This is the way to go that all activities take after a curve or a somewhat roundabout way. The special cases to this tenet are the livelinesss of mechanical gadgets or contraptions. Curves make a significantly more regular and streaming development and are especially essential when energizing the human figure or the activities of a creature. All body developments, from the swinging of an arm to the turning of a head, portray a curve through space. In light of this it is most advantageous to consider any regular development like the swinging of a pendulum.

3.2.2.8 Secondary activity

This kind of activity is utilized to improve and upgrade the fundamental activity. It can elevate the feeling or mind-set of a character liveliness, adding another measurement to the execution. These activities are regularly exceptionally unobtrusive with the point of complimenting or expanding the effect of the fundamental activity. The auxiliary activities would include whatever other activities that bolster and expand the characters feeling of wretchedness.
They may incorporate a substantial quieting of the head, a sensational and sorrowful murmur or an occupied kick at something in the way. In the event that the characters walk is his primary activity, then all different activities of the body are auxiliary or supporting activity.

3.2.2.9 Timing

'Timing is the piece of liveliness that offers intending to development' Timing is one of the hardest components of movement to get perfectly fine characterizes the pace at which all the activities happen. Some extremely fundamental thoughts can be highlighted. They are basically that the more drawings put between postures makes a moderate and smooth activity though less drawings make the activity speedier and smart. Most activity is done on twos (one drawing records for 2 casings of film) and are utilized at whatever point conceivable, sparing a great deal of work. More unobtrusive or quicker activities are vivified on ones (one drawing for every edge of film). Likewise, cautious timing must be considered when a character is acting with a specific end goal to create disposition and feeling. At the point when fusing the utilization of intricate optional activities and covering development it is anything but difficult to perceive how entangled vivifying can get to be as every individual component of the shot will need to be timed independently. On the off chance that one component is timed ineffectively then the whole scene would fall flat regardless of how well everything else functioned. Hence there is no other route for an artist to learn timing activities effectively than to take a seat and deal with it through experimentation.

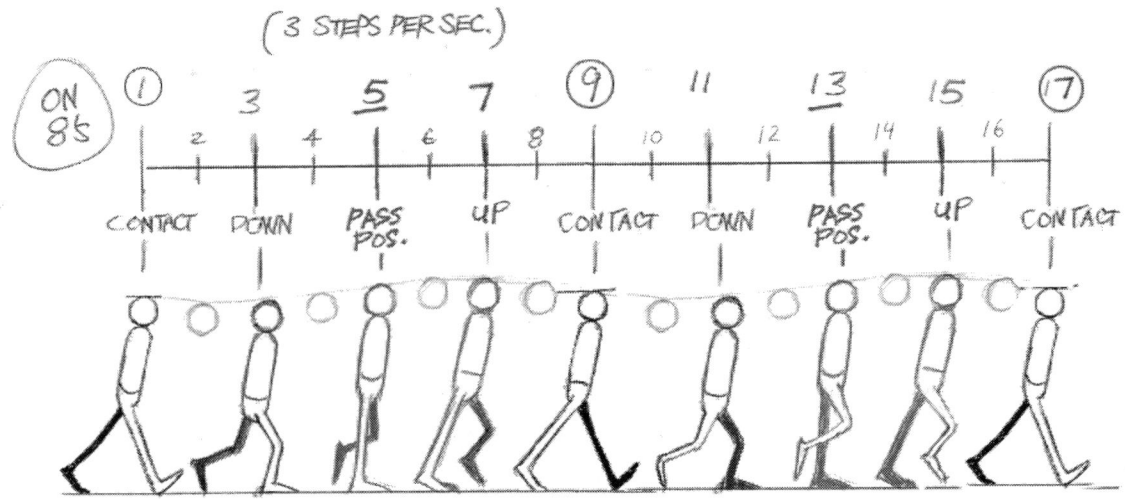

Fig 3.2.2.9: timing is maintained according to the sequence of scene and motion.

3.2.2.10 Exaggeration

Embellishment intends to concentrate the substance of an activity and improve it to make it additionally persuading. On the off chance that an activity from a real to life film was basically followed onto paper and played back as a movement, the outcome would be an extremely inflexible and vacant execution. To make development more regular it needs to be more extensive with more accentuation on the facial highlights, articulations, postures and mentality. Candid and Ollie depict it as the measure of embellishment shifts relying upon the style of activity being made. A short cartoon will contain inordinate measures of distortion for an all the more in your face result.

Fig 3.2.2.10: Extracting of an action to enhance and make it more convincing.

3.2.2.11 Solid Drawing

Under control drawn activity this is presumably the most clear and basic rule to handle. In place for a liveliness to work it must be drawn well. Drawings ought to have weight, profundity, equalization and the various fundamental angles used to make the hallucination of strong, three dimensional shapes on paper. Additionally, when assembled as an enlivened grouping, the drawings must cooperate and structure the hallucination of fourth-dimensional life. The fourth measurement is development in time.

3.2.2.12 Appeal

This is to make a character configuration or an activity that the gathering of people will appreciate viewing. Advance comes to fruition through effortlessness of configuration, clear drawing and the advancement of an identity that will dazzle and interest the group of onlookers. Each character, whether courageous, insidious, comic or adorable ought to have request.

3.2.3 STORY FOR THE ANIMATION MOVIE

Movement is about story and outflow of character. For making a decent activity there ought to be a decent story and declaration. In making of any liveliness 1st we select the story then characters, representations, and in the wake of organizing every edge of film we try for music or verses if there are dialogs then we portray the story from the view of topic or any character of the motion picture.

3.2.4 Character designing and their value in animation

Characters are everything you need after when you are done with the story. We have to design the character according to requirement of the story and give them according to their value or their character in the story. Different character, in a particular scene, their expression and how they in a particular scene.

Fig 3.2.5.1: Change in character value when beard is added, which gives it the value of a grown person.

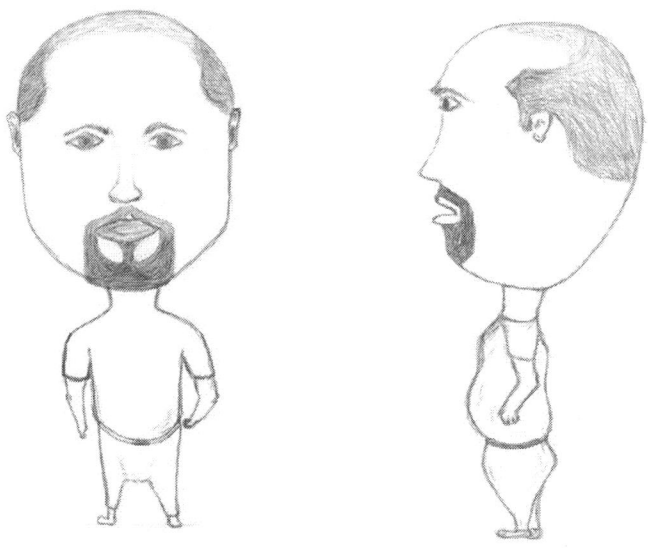

Fig 3.2.5.2: Front view and side view of character.

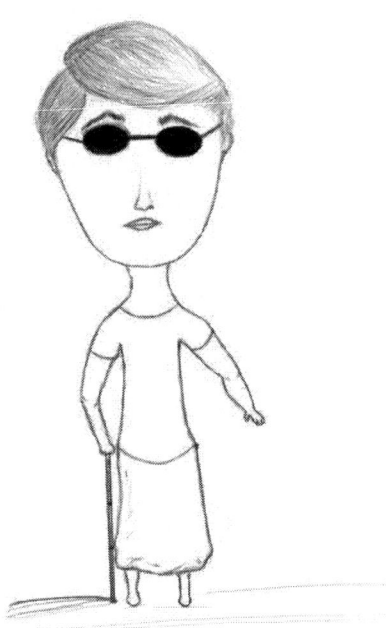

Fig 3.2.5.3: blind person with dark specs showing the loss of vision with no expression on face.

Fig 3.2.5.4: Girl character, showing a little value as a young and innocent person.

Fig 3.2.5.5: Square mentioned in the story and traffic signal.

3.3 Cognitive behaviour of students using animation as a learning tool

Cognitive conduct of an individual uncommonly an understudy while learning lets us know about his fixation, his advantage towards the subject and the way he approaches towards the subject. This conduct lets us know that whether individual is taking interest or not while being a piece of the class. With exploration done in this cognitive conduct region we saw that understudies who are the piece of the classroom program, things are taught by an educator by simply clarifying the point orally or by specifying the critical focuses by composing it on the board. However in our hypothesis when understudies are taught the themes by clarifying them with the assistance of pictures, design shaded or not and by films or ought to say liveliness there are couple of things we recognized which demonstrate that somehow understudies are more focusing on subjects than before and they are creating the nature of imaging the things. Understudies are presently understanding things better and their learning effectiveness is additionally expanded yet it likewise fluctuate with the representation of movement, the quality educating with showing distinctive themes with things like liveliness and shading illustrations.

3.4   colours significance in illustrations planning

Shading in configuration is exceptionally subjective. What brings out one response in one individual may bring out an altogether different response in another person. Here and there this is because of individual inclination, and different times because of social foundation. Shading hypothesis is a science in itself. Concentrating on how hues influence distinctive individuals, either exclusively or as a gathering, is something a few individuals assemble their vocations on. Something as basic as changing the accurate tint or immersion of a shading can bring out a totally diverse feeling. Social contrasts imply that something that is cheerful and elevating in one nation can be discouraging in another.

The significance of hues differing from the same essential shading with some differentiation may look same however in utilizing it with different hues may characterize things in other way. Couple of illustrations of shading wonder which characterizes how essential shading vary from its optional with a slight change interestingly.

Warm Colors:

Fig 3.4.1: warm colours.

Warm hues incorporate red, orange, and yellow, and varieties of those three hues. These are the shades of flame, of fall leaves, and of dusks and day breaks, and are for the most part stimulating, energetic, and positive. Red and yellow are both essential hues, with orange falling in the center, which means warm hues are all really warm and aren't made by joining a warm shading with a cool shading. Utilize warm hues as a part of your outlines to reflect energy, satisfaction, eagerness, and vitality.

Red (primary colour):

Fig 3.4.2: Red (primary colour).

Red is an extremely hot shading. It's connected with flame, roughness, and fighting. It's additionally connected with affection and energy. Ever, it's been connected with both the Devil and Cupid. Red can really have a physical impact on individuals, raising pulse and breath rates. It's been demonstrated to improve human digestion system, as well. Red can be connected with indignation, but on the other hand is connected with significance (think about celebrity main street at recompenses shows and big name occasions). Red likewise demonstrates peril (the reason stop lights and signs are red, and that most cautioning marks are red). In distinctive piece of globe in diverse nations definition and importance of hues is diverse. Outside the western world, red has distinctive affiliations. For instance, in China, red is the shading of flourishing and joy and used to pull in good fortunes.

Eastern societies, red is worn by ladies on their wedding days. In South Africa, then again, red is the shading of grieving. Red is likewise connected with socialism. Red has turned into the shading connected with AIDS mindfulness in Africa.

Orange (secondary color):

Fig 3.4.3: Orange (secondary colour).

Orange is an exceptionally energetic and vivacious shading. In its quieted structures, it can be connected with the earth and with fall. Due to its relationship with the evolving seasons, orange can speak to change and development by and large. Since orange is connected with the product of the same name, it can be connected with wellbeing and essentialness. In plans, orange orders consideration without being as overwhelming as red. It's frequently viewed as all the more amicable and welcoming, and less in-your-face.

Fig 3.4.4: dark orange picture in lime green background.

In this picture we see the dark orange, when set against the lime green, almost acts as a neutral and grounding color here.

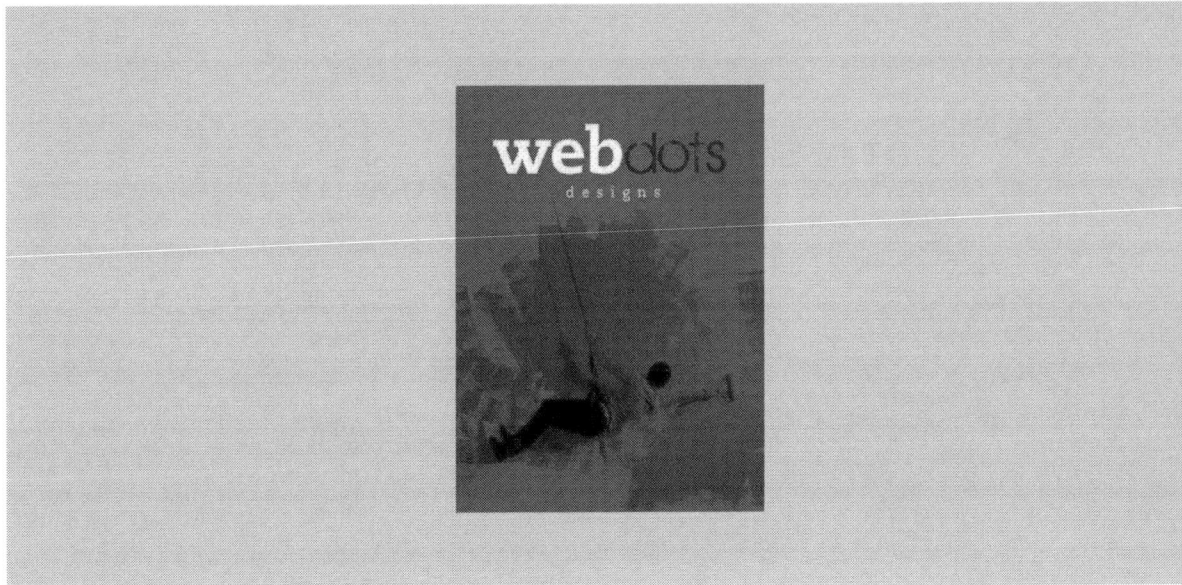

Fig 3.4.5: dark orange picture in pink background.

Same pic shown above in lime green background when shown in light pink background it appears to be coming out. Background doesn't attract the viewer.

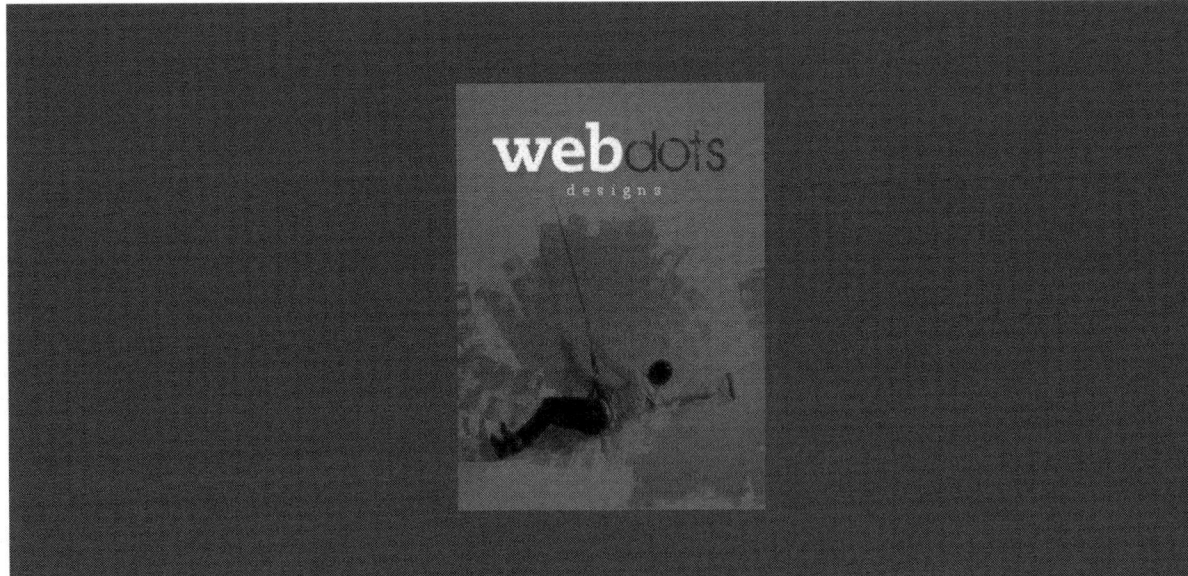

Fig 3.34.6: dark orange picture in dark red background.

In this picture image at centre looks like a printed image on a solid background. Background is solid and both image and background here amusing the viewer.

Cool Colors:

Fig 3.4.7: Cool colours.

Cool hues incorporate green, blue, and purple, are frequently more quelled than warm hues. They are the shades of night, of water, of nature, and are typically cooling, unwinding, and to a degree saved. Blue is the main essential shading inside the cool range, which implies alternate hues are made by consolidating blue with a warm shading (yellow for green and red for purple). Greens tackle a percentage of the characteristics of yellow, and purple tackles a portion of the traits of red. Utilization cool hues in your outlines to give a feeling of quiet or demonstrable skill.

Yellow(primarycolor):

Fig 3.4.8: Yellow (primary colour).

Yellow is regularly viewed as the brightest and most invigorating of the warm hues. It's connected with joy and daylight. Yellow can likewise be connected with misdirection and sassiness, however (calling somebody yellow is calling them a whiney little girl). Yellow is additionally connected with trust, as can be seen in a few nations when yellow strips are shown by families who have friends and family at war. Yellow is additionally connected with risk, however not as unequivocally as red.

Green(secondarycolor):

Fig 3.4.9: Green (secondary colour).

Green is a sensible shading. It can speak to fresh starts and development. It additionally implies recharging and plenitude. Then again, green can likewise speak to envy or desire, and an absence of experience. Green has a significant number of the same smoothing characteristics that blue has, however it likewise fuses a portion of the vitality of yellow. In outline, green can have an adjusting and fitting impact, and is exceptionally steady. It's suitable for outlines identified with riches, soundness, replenishment, and nature. Brighter greens are additionally empowering and lively, while olive greens are more illustrative of the common world. Dim greens are the most steady and illustrative of riches.

Blue(primarycolor):

Fig 3.4.10: Blue(primarycolor)

Blue is frequently connected with pity in the English dialect. Blue is likewise utilized broadly to speak to tranquility and obligation. Light soul can be reviving and cordial. Dull soul are more solid and dependable. Blue is likewise connected with peace, and has profound and religious meanings in numerous societies and customs (for instance, the Virgin Mary is for the most part portrayed wearing blue robes).

The significance of blue is generally influenced relying upon the accurate shade and tone. In plan, the precise shade of blue you select will have a tremendous effect on how your outlines are seen. Light soul are frequently casual and smoothing. Splendid soul can be stimulating and reviving. Dim soul are incredible for corporate locales or plans where quality and dependability are essential.

Purple(secondarycolor):

Fig 3.4.11: Purple (secondary color)

Purple was since a long time ago connected with eminence. It's a blend of red and blue, and tackles a few traits of both. It's connected with innovativeness and creative energy, as well. In Thailand, purple is the shading of grieving for widows. Dim purples are generally connected with riches and eminence, while lighter purples are viewed as more sentimental. In configuration, dull purples can give a sense riches and extravagance. Light purples are gentler and are connected with spring and sentiment.

Neutral colours:

Fig 3.4.12: Neutral colours

Purple was since a long time ago connected with eminence. It's a blend of red and blue, and tackles a few traits of both. It's connected with innovativeness and creative energy, as well. In Thailand, purple is the shading of grieving for widows. Dim purples are generally connected with riches and eminence, while lighter purples are viewed as more sentimental. In configuration, dull purples can give a sense riches and extravagance. Light purples are gentler and are connected with spring and sentiment.

Black : Strongest neutral colour

Fig 3.4.13 : Black : Strongest neutral colour

Dark is the strongest of the nonpartisan hues. On the positive side, it's usually connected with force, tastefulness, and convention. On the negative side, it can be connected with underhandedness, demise, and secret. Dark is the conventional shading of grieving in numerous Western nations. It's additionally connected with defiance in a few societies, and is connected with Halloween and the mysterious.

3.5 Psychological properties of colours

There are four mental essential hues red, blue, yellow and green. They relate individually to the body, the brain, the feelings and the vital harmony between these three.
The mental properties of the eleven essential hues are as per the following:

RED: Physical

Fig 3.5.1: RED, Physical

Positive: Physical valor, quality, warmth, vitality, essential survival, 'battle or flight', incitement, manliness, energy.

Negative: Defiance, hostility, visual effect, strain.

Being the longest wavelength, red is an effective shading. Albeit not actually the most unmistakable, it has the property of seeming, by all accounts, to be closer than it is and in this way it gets our consideration first. Subsequently its adequacy in activity lights the world over. Its impact is physical; it animates us and raises the beat rate, giving the feeling that time is passing speedier than it is. It identifies with the manly rule and can actuate the "battle or flight" sense. Red is solid, and exceptionally fundamental. Immaculate red is the easiest shading, with no nuance. It is animating and enthusiastic, agreeable. In the meantime, it can be seen as requesting and forceful.

BLUE. Intellectual.

Fig 3.5.2: BLUE. Intellectual

Positive: Intelligence, correspondence, trust, effectiveness, quietness, obligation, rationale, coolness, reflection, smooth.

Negative: Coldness, aloofness, absence of feeling, unpleasantness.

Blue is the shading of the psyche and is basically calming. It influences us rationally, instead of the physical response we need to red. Solid soul will empower clear thought and lighter, delicate soul will quiet the brain and help focus. Hence it is tranquil and rationally smoothing. It is the shading of clear correspondence. Blue items don't seem, by all accounts, to be as near to us as red ones. Over and over in exploration, blue is the world's most loved shading. In any case, it can be seen as icy, unemotional and unpleasant.

YELLOW. Emotional

Fig 3.5.3: YELLOW. Emotional

Positive: Optimism, certainty, respect toward oneself, extraversion, passionate quality, amicability, inventiveness.

Negative: Irrationality, dread, enthusiastic delicacy, discouragement, uneasiness, suicide.

The yellow wavelength is moderately long and basically fortifying. For this situation the boost is passionate, accordingly yellow is the strongest shading, mentally. The right yellow will lift our spirits and our respect toward oneself. It is the shading of certainty and hopefulness. Excessively of it, or the wrong tone in connection to alternate tones in a shading plan, can result in respect toward oneself to plunge, offering ascent to trepidation and tension. Our "yellow streak" can surface.

GREEN. Balance

Fig 3.5.4: Green. Balance

Positive: Harmony, equalization, refreshment, all inclusive adoration, rest, rebuilding, consolation, natural mindfulness, balance, peace.

Negative: Boredom, stagnation, flatness, enervation.

Green strikes the eye so as to oblige no change whatever and is serene. Being in the inside of the range, it is the shading of parity a more essential idea than numerous individuals figure it out. At the point when the world about us contains a lot of green, this demonstrates the vicinity of water, and minimal threat of starvation, so we are consoled by green, on a primitive level. Adversely, it can demonstrate stagnation and, erroneously utilized, will be seen as being excessively tasteless.

VIOLET. Spiritual

Fig 3.5.5: VIOLET. Spiritual

Positive: Spiritual mindfulness, regulation, vision, extravagance, credibility, truth, quality.

Negative: Introversion, debauchery, concealment, inadequacy.

The most limited wavelength is violet, regularly portrayed as purple. It takes attention to a larger amount of thought, even into the domains of profound qualities. It is profoundly introvertive and empowers profound consideration, or contemplation. It has relationship with sovereignty and ordinarily imparts the finest conceivable quality. Being the last obvious wavelength before the bright beam, it has relationship with time and space and the universe. Exorbitant utilization of purple can realize an excessive amount of reflection and the wrong tone of it imparts something shabby and awful, quicker than some other shading.

ORANGE.

Fig 3.5.6: Orange

Positive: Physical solace, nourishment, warmth, security, arousing quality, energy, wealth, fun.

Negative: Deprivation, disappointment, pointlessness, youthfulness.

Since it is a mix of red and yellow, orange is empowering and response to it is a mix of the physical and the enthusiastic. It centers our brains on issues of physical solace nourishment, warmth, cover and so forth and arousing quality. It is a "fun" shading. Contrarily, it may concentrate on the definite inverse hardship. This is especially likely when warm orange is utilized with dark. Similarly, an excess of orange proposes pointlessness and an absence of genuine learned qualities.

PINK.

Fig 3.5.7: Pink

Positive: Physical serenity, support, warmth, womanliness, love, sexuality, survival of the species.

Negative: Inhibition, enthusiastic claustrophobia, castration, physical shortcoming.

Being a tint of red, pink likewise influences us physically, however it mitigates, instead of animates. (Interestingly, red is the main shading that has a totally separate name for its tints. Tints of blue, green, yellow, and so on are essentially called light blue, light green and so forth.) Pink is a capable colour, mentally. It speaks to the female guideline, and survival of the species. It is supporting and physically mitigating. An excessive amount of pink is physically depleting and can be to a degree weakening.

GREY.

Fig 3.5.8: Grey

Positive: Psychological impartiality.

Negative: Lack of certainty, sogginess, dejection, hibernation, absence of vitality.

Immaculate dark is the main shading that has no direct mental properties. It is, on the other hand, very suppressive. A virtual unlucky deficiency of shading is discouraging and when the world turns dim we are intuitively molded to attract and plan for hibernation. Unless the exact tone is correct, dim has a hosing impact on different hues utilized with it. Overwhelming utilization of dim as a rule shows an absence of certainty and apprehension of introduction.

BLACK.

Fig 3.5.9: Black

Positive: Sophistication, charm, security, passionate wellbeing, productivity, substance.

Negative: Oppression, coldness, hazard, largeness.

Dark is all hues, completely ingested. The mental ramifications of that are significant. It makes defensive hindrances, as it assimilates all the vitality impending towards you, and it conceals the identity. Dark is basically an unlucky deficiency of light, since no wavelengths are reflected and it can, in this way be threatening. Numerous individuals are perplexed about the dim. Emphatically, it conveys outright clarity, with no fine subtleties. It imparts advancement and uncompromising brilliance and it lives up to expectations especially well with white. Dark makes an impression of weight and earnestness. It is a myth that dark garments are thinning. Reality behind the myth is that dark is the most latent shading a matter of not attracting thoughtfulness regarding yourself, instead of really making you look slimmer.

WHITE.

Fig 3.5.10: White

Positive: Hygiene, sterility, clarity, virtue, cleanness, effortlessness, modernity, effectiveness.

Negative: Sterility, coldness, boundaries, unpleasantness, elitism.

Generally as dark is downright assimilation, so white is complete reflection. In actuality, it mirrors the full drive of the range at us. In this way it likewise makes boundaries, yet uniquely in contrast to dark, and it is regularly a strain to take a gander at. It conveys, "Touch me not!" White is virtue and, in the same way as dark, uncompromising; it is clean, hygienic, and sterile. The idea of sterility can likewise be negative. Outwardly, white gives an increased impression of space. The negative impact of white on warm hues is to make them look and feel gaudy.

BROWN.

Fig 3.5.11: Brown

Positive: Seriousness, warmth, Nature, heartiness, dependability, support.

Negative: Lack of diversion, largeness, absence of complexity.

Cocoa typically comprises of red and yellow, with a huge rate of dark. Hence, it has a significant part of the same earnestness as dark, however is hotter and gentler. It has components of the red and yellow properties. Cocoa has relationship with the earth and the characteristic world. It is a strong, solid shading and the vast majority discover it discreetly steady more emphatically than the ever prominent dark, which is suppressive, as opposed to strong.

3.6 Perceptual salience vs Thematic Relevance

Many-sided quality of the topic may not be the main explanation behind troubles that learners now and then have with activitys. It appears that issues can likewise emerge from the perceptual impacts of such presentations. In an inadequately composed activity, the data that learners perceive most promptly in the liveliness may not be the data that is of most prominent significance. Then again, data that is generally unnoticeable may be imperative. Clearly, detectable quality of data does not so much compare with its real pertinence to the learning assignment to be performed. Highlights of the energized showcase that are most arresting in view of their appear differently in relation to whatever remains of the presentation are not generally the best place for learners to direct their consideration. As it were, there can be a poor correspondence between the perceptual notability ('recognisability') of a highlight and its topical significance, and a going hand in hand with content is expected to revise this.

This correspondence issue can happen with both static and vivified design. On a simply perceptual level, our consideration has a tendency to be pulled in by a few sections of a static show more than by different parts because of their visuospatial properties. For instance, an article that is midway set, moderately expansive, abnormally molded, and of a pointedly differentiating shading or surface is prone to 'hop out' of the showcase so we perceive it effectively. Different things in the showcase may get correspondingly less consideration thus.

Decently outlined static instructive design exploit these perceptual impacts. They control the attributes of the presentation keeping in mind the end goal to direct learner consideration regarding the most pertinent data. This serves to guarantee that the learner will remove the obliged data from the presentation. There is an issue in the configuration of the liveliness demonstrated above in this admiration. Lamentably, there are numerous "instructive" illustrations being delivered that neglect to furnish learners with sufficient backing of this sort. Planners of liveliness need to consider such thought.

3.7 Composition of images in animation.

In traditional way of making the animation we basically focus on the character part and making the frames part to give motion to our character. We don't follow any specific rules to make our picture more attractive or to make it such that it focuses more at some point but as a part of whole picture. That particular portion or point should be emerging out of the whole picture. With our research on making character and on making animation by composition of images or frames we came to know about basic simple 9 factors which if followed can be a great asset in designing the graphics and animation for educational purpose.

1. Place point of interests on intersection.

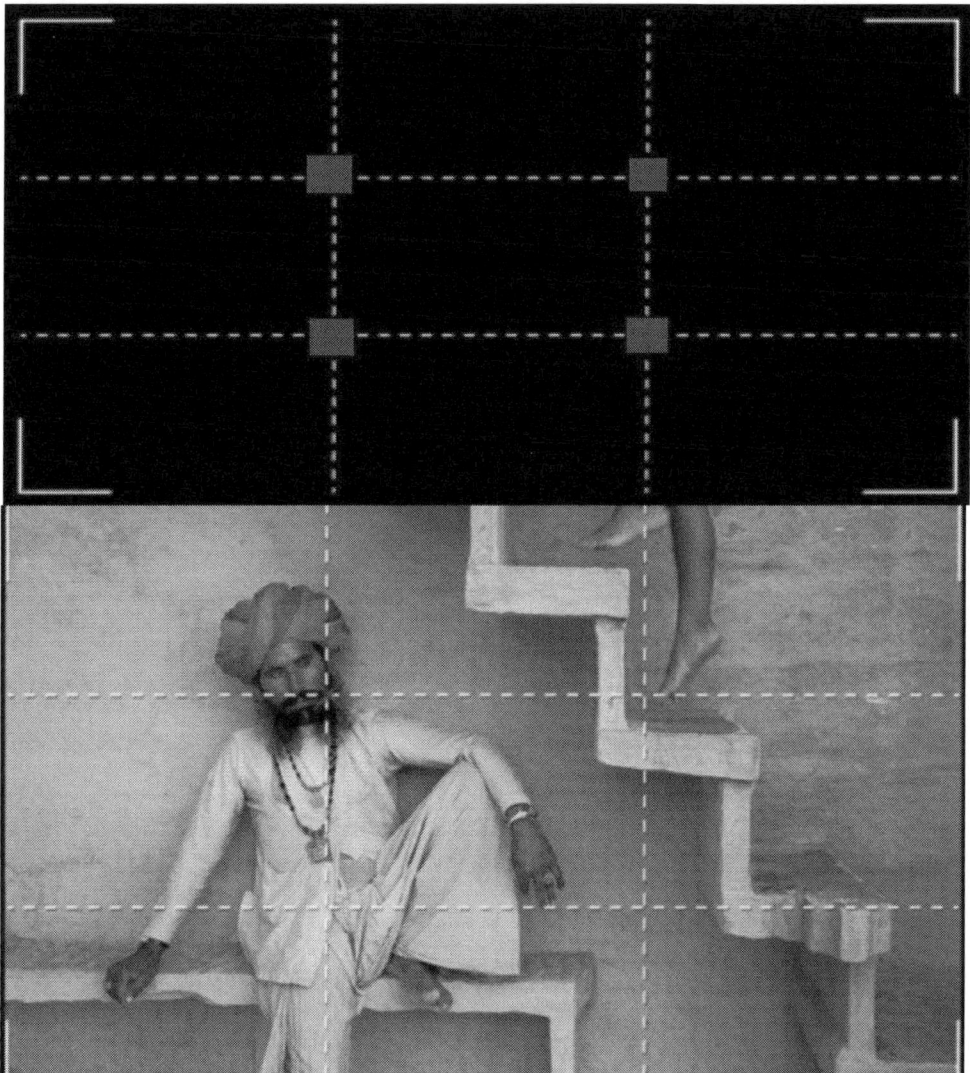

Fig 3.7.1: intersecting lines

In picture person with beard is the first thing we look at. If we see the lines drawn so it is at intersection of one of the four intersection points.

2. Position important elements along the lines

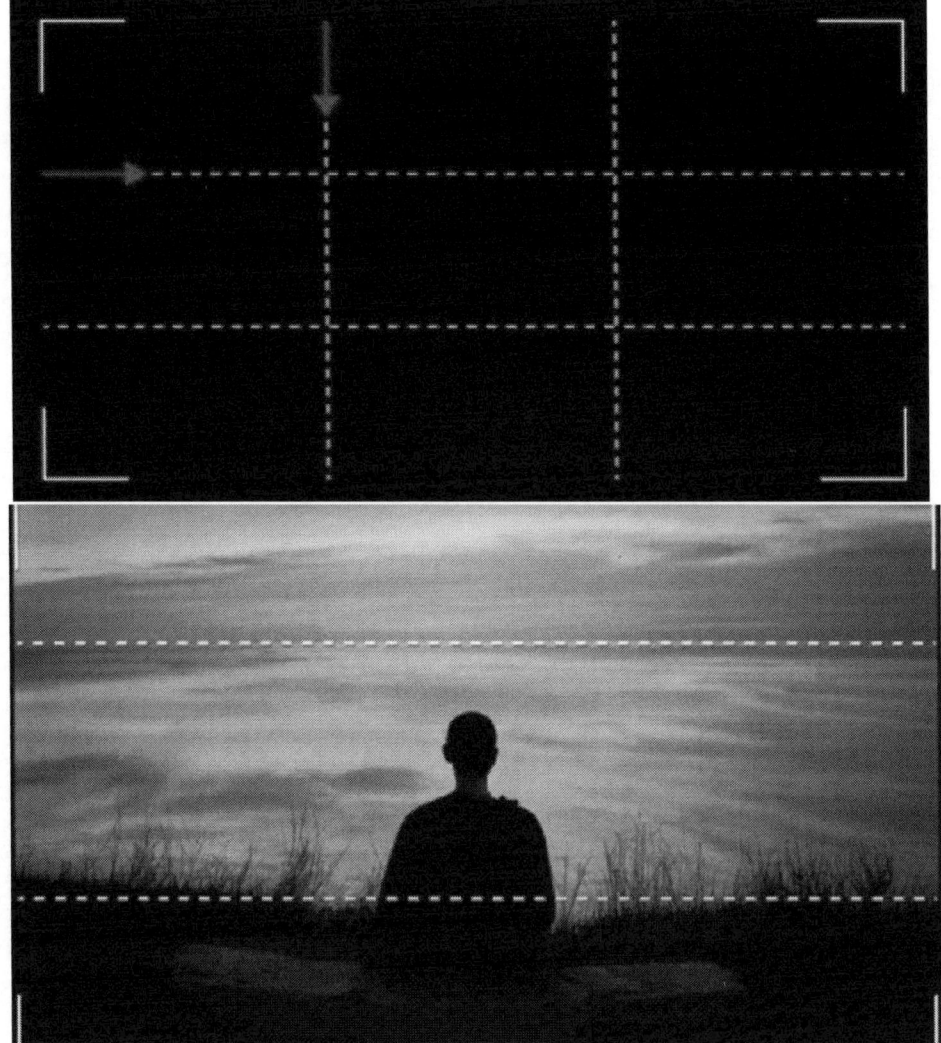
Fig 3.7.2: element along the lines.

3. Use natural lines to lead the eye into the picture

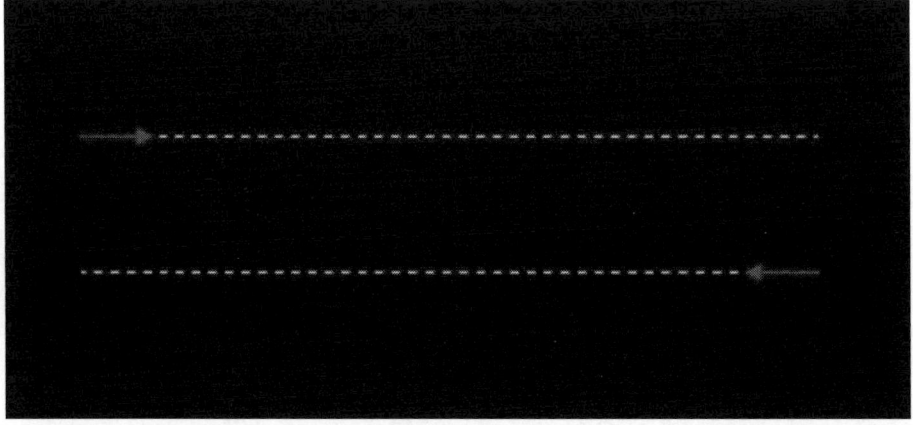

Fig 3.7.3: natural lines.

3 Diagonal lines create great movement

Fig 3.7.4: diagonal lines.

4   Use natural frames like windows and doors

Fig 3.7.5: natural frames.

5   Find contrast between subject and background

Fig 3.7.6: contrast between subject and background.

6   Fill the frames get close to your subjects

Place the dominant eye in the centre of the photo

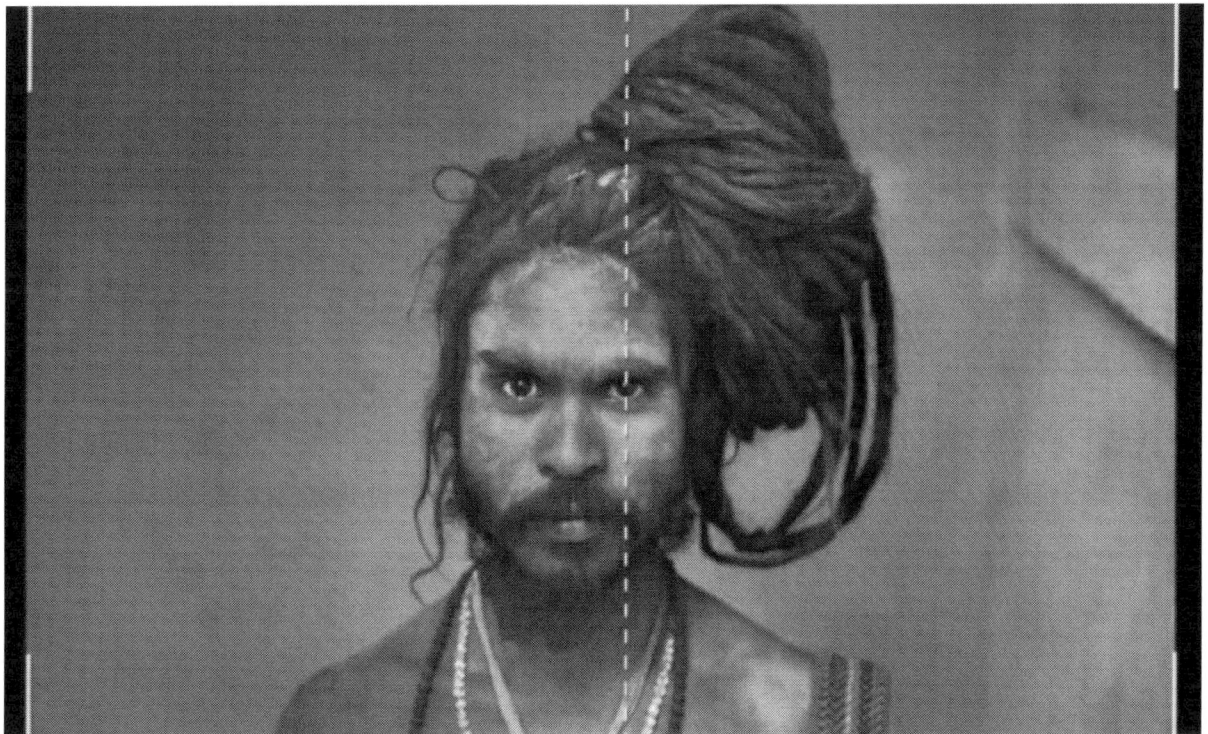
Fig 3.7.7: closer look at frame.

This gives the impression the eyes follows you.

7 Patterns and repetition

Fig 3.7.8: Patterns and repetition

Patterns are aesthetically pleasing but best is when pattern is interrupted.

Fig 3.7.9: interrupted pattern.

8   Symmetry: pleasing to eye

Fig 3.7.10: symmetry

3.8 Detail procedure for animating the story

Detail procedure includes the story, software adobe flash.

3.8.1 Story

In this scene all the students are inside the class and teacher comes inside the class and write on the black board "SURPRISE TEST". Teacher goes to everyone and gives the question paper. In question paper there a boy see the pair matching questions and see that they are very easy and start answering them. Boy comes to a question in which he see that he has to pair men and eyes with corresponding picture and after thinking for some time and about the blind person he matches the eyes for men and men for eye.
So basic motto of this story to tell the people that people with no vision need it while many with these avoid a lot of things in their daily life.

3.8.2 Adobe flash: Animation software

Adobe flash is an animation software used to make animation with adobe tools or with the graphics generated in flash or by importing the images from other sources and then using the frames to create the animation. Animation can be created as a single frame or multiple frame animation.

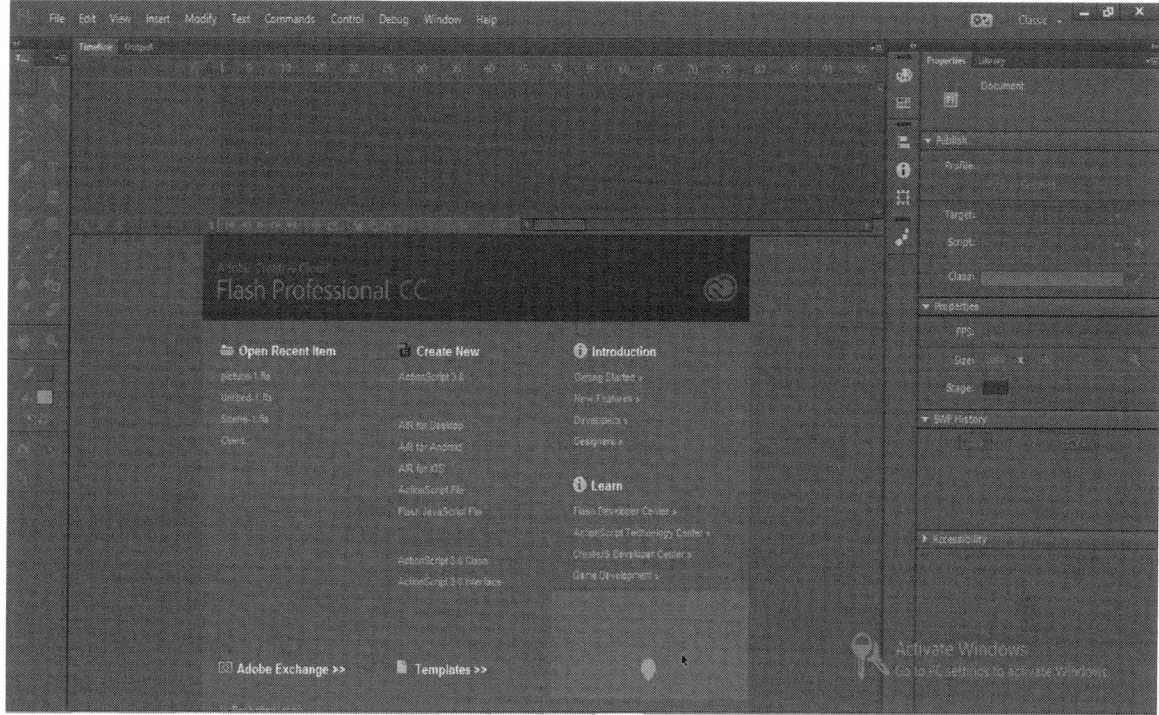

Fig 3.8.2.1: Adobe flash layout.

ActionScript 3.0 is the platform on which animation movies are made. It's an inbuilt coded platform on which there is no need of coding. By using adobe tools we do design the characters and move them across the background to create animation.

Adobe flash ActionScript 3.0

Fig 3.8.2.2: adobe flash ActionScript 3.0 screen.

Adobe flash tools:

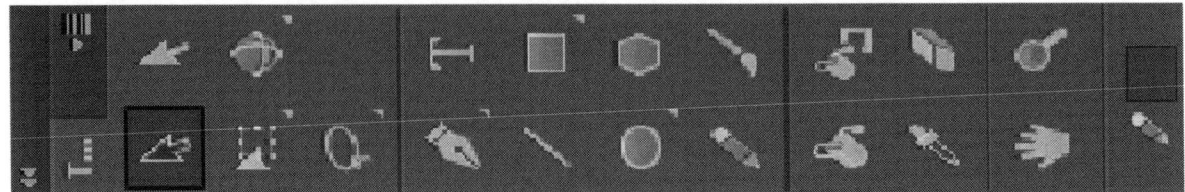

Fig 3.8.2.3: adobe tools

Arrow (Selection Tool): This is utilized for at whatever point you are not utilizing any of alternate apparatuses. It chooses individual protests or edges or a marquee for selecting different items. It works the device bar and menu frameworks. And so forth.

Sub selection Tool: used to select the whole structure.

Brush: The Brush instrument is much the same as the pencil yet it permits you to make thicker items for freehand drawing.

Dropper: Use the eyedropper instrument to duplicate fill and stroke qualities from one shape or line and promptly apply them to another shape or line.

Eraser: Pretty self-explanatory really.

Lasso: This is utilized for selecting single or numerous articles in difficult to achieve puts by permitting you to draw a line, which then turns into the choice.

Line: This device does what the title recommends. It draws lines. Valuable for drawing polygons and other abnormal shapes the Oval and Rectangle apparatuses can't manage.

Pen Tool: Allows you to draw extremely exact lines vector lines and bends for filling.

Magnifier: You will have the capacity to zoom in on your stage and articles with this apparatus. Holding down the "Alt" key will change the pointer to a "short" sign. This will empower you to zoom out.

Paint Bucket: This will fill objects with a shading of your picking. Ink Bottle: This instrument makes lines around articles. Case in point, in the wake of selecting the instrument and clicking on a circle object it will make a round line around it. This can then be transform into a different item.

Pencil: This device draws freehand lines. Some splendid flashes at Macromedia have allowed you the capacity to straighten and smooth the assaults of your shaky hand. Have a play with this by picking Modify> Curves> …

Rectangle: Another helpful apparatus and you got it! It draws squares. When you draw one it will make a fringe as well in the event that you need to outskirt shading chose. Clicking on the outskirt once and it will just highlight one side. A twofold click will highlight each of the four sides. Oval: An exceptionally valuable instrument, which permits the originator to make circles and ovals of any size. Keep in mind: When you draw an oval, Flash makes an outskirt around it in the event that you have a fringe shading chosen. So in the event that you don't need it there either kill the fringe shading or click on the outskirt of the item, this will highlight the outskirt, and erase it.

Text: This apparatus permits the fashioner to make content or content fields. Fill Transform device; Adjusts the course and edge of an angle or bitmap fill.

Free Transform tool: Allows you to pivot, scale or skew a chose object.

Hand Tool: Allows you to rapidly move around the stage.

Deco Tool: Fills the stage with irritating examples, helpful for practically... nothing!

3D Rotation Tool: Exactly what it recommends however won't be required right.

Timeline: in this section we use layers to generate the images on background just like we are making them on background and then we add frames in these layers to give the pause at particular scene. At the bottom of timeline buttons are given to generate new layer and according to our need we can set the time elapsed in each frame.

Fig 3.8.2.4: Adobe flash timeline

There are 3 types of frames keyframe
- Keyframe
- Regular frame
- Blank keyframe

Shortcut for inserting and deleting these frames.
F6- to insert keyframe
F5- to insert regular frames
F7- to insert blank keyframe
Shift + F5- to delete frames
Shift + F6- to delete keyframe

3.9 Result

Fig 3.9: final figure

CONCLUSION

This thesis investigate the methods or principal need to follow and how one can produce error free animation or graphics if he follow the principles. And with the help of the new techniques, principle and graphics and animation designing software we can make animation a good learning tool for students and others. We tried and design the characters for our story and gave them the look which fit for our story and which with we can continue to give the expression when we give them motion. And after studying the literature and doing practice on adobe flash and other animation software we came to know that to make a good animation one should have proper skills. Any person can make an animation movie but for that someone need to be good in understanding the graphics and psychology behind the colour theory. And if with good understanding of colours and composition of images and points which we found are very important in designing graphics and animation can be a very good asset in making animation a good learning tool.

Printed in Great Britain
by Amazon

35160599R00024